"There is no better than adversity. Every defeat, every heartbreak, every loss, contains its own seed, its own lesson on how to improve your performance next time."

-Malcolm X

This book is dedicated to my family, my babies (students), and Ms. Adams.

Thanks for seeing me when I didn't see myself!

You will become a better person because you want to.

No matter your past, you are worth the fight to overcome every negative thought that tries to capture your mind and hold you hostage to fear!

You are an overcomer…
Not just any overcomer…

You are the overcomer that is going to change the lives of others who experience hardships just like the ones in your past.

You are not a mistake.

You are the chosen one.

Walk in Love!

-April

Table of Contents

Part 1: Who Am I?   **Pg. 7**

Part 2: Walk in Self-Love   **Pg. 35**

Part 3: Healthy Relationships   **Pg. 55**

Closing: Walk in Prosperity   **Pg. 79**

Introduction

It is with great joy and honor that I write this book. For far too long, people have told stories of our youth not having day to day issues due to their "inexperience" in life. Well, that time has come to an end.

Most of the issues that I have encountered in my adulthood manifested due to issues deeply rooted in my adolescent years. Many of my peers would say the same. Therefore, it is my mission to help prevent the impact of childhood trauma in adulthood by providing necessary tools presented in a growth mindset format.

How to Use This Book?

"Mirror, Mirror" is an interactive book. Therefore, you must put in work to reap the benefits of it.

As you go through this book, annotate what applies to your life by highlighting or underlining what stands out.

Remember to say your affirmations while looking in the mirror or say them out loud in the morning, midday, and night.

*** I write mine on my mirror and sticky notes to help keep them in sight.

Also, remember to complete each reflection and journal prompt.

This will help you prioritize problems, solutions, and areas of growth.

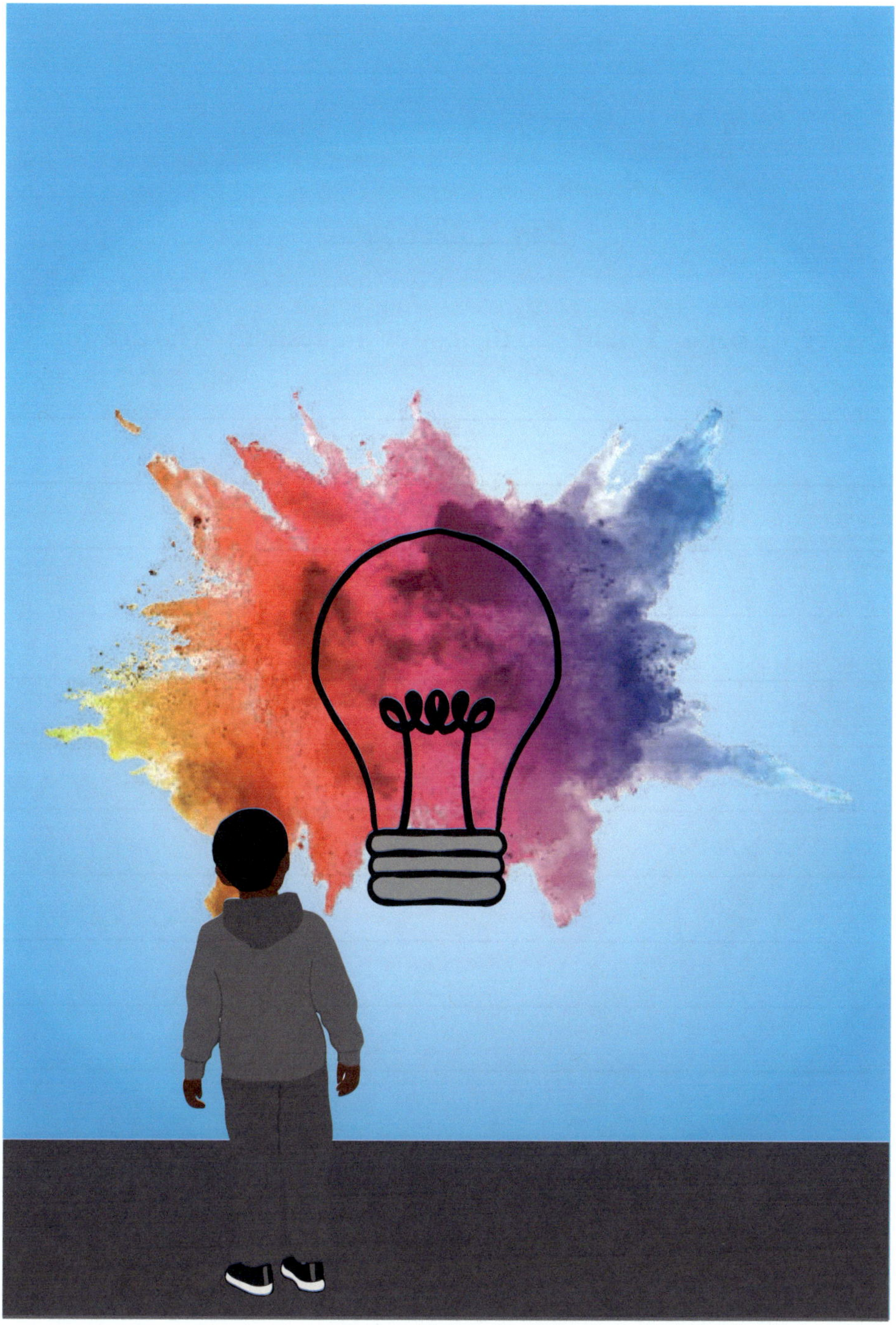

Part 1: Who Am I?

Before we begin, I want you to answer a question: Who are you?

_____

_____

_____

_____

_____

_____

_____

_____

_____

_____

_____

_____

Wondering why did I ask you this question? Well, when answering it for the first time, my initial response included my name, age, and career. However, those things do not define what I stand for or my beliefs.

Check out the Self-Awareness Guide below and answer the question using the sentence stems as a guide.

For example: I am a happy and loving person. I am the happiest when I help people grow to become better than before.

Self-Awareness Guide:

I am a…
My strengths are…
My limitations are… I can improve them by…
I am the happiest when…
I am hurt when…
I am passionate about…
With no outside influences, I enjoy…
My purpose on Earth is…
I want to improve my life by…
I love myself because…

Let's Put in Work!

Think about the Self-Awareness Guide and answer the question more in depth in the space below.

_____
_____
_____
_____
_____
_____
_____
_____
_____
_____
_____

Understanding who you are as a person leads to self-discovery. Knowing your identity or who you are as an individual is super important. It is ultimately the reason you make certain choices in your life. My high school principal had a favorite saying, "Every decision you make has a consequence, you determine whether the consequence is positive or negative by the choices you make." I graduated some time ago, yet I remind myself daily to make the best choices for my life.

Cleansing

I am so proud of you for making it to the next steps. Now that you've identified yourself as an individual, let's cleanse ourselves of negative thoughts. I personally do this every single day!

Begin by looking in the mirror. Now, say five positive things you like about yourself.

Here are my five:

1. I like that I am optimistic.
2. I like my smile.
3. I like my ability to motivate others.
4. I like that I'm a spontaneous person.
5. I like that I overcome obstacles.

**Your turn! List five things you like about yourself.
Good vibes only!**

1. _____

2. _____

3. _____

4. _____

5. _____

Awesome job!

Now, let's develop our **daily affirmations**.

Your assignment is to **CREATE** customized affirmations
to help you think positive thoughts.

This activity will help us change the way we think, which will ultimately change our lives.

For best results, read them in the morning, noon, and night.

Here's an example on how to develop your affirmations.

I listed three areas I'd like to change in my life.
1. I can improve my life by setting boundaries
2. I can increase my workout plan.
3. I can accept when people leave my life.

Next, I wrote the positive opposite of each:

Affirmations:
1. I know myself and honor the healthy boundaries I've set for a happy life.
2. I crush all my fitness goals.
3. I am worthy of the right people entering my life so that I know their stay is beneficial.

YOUR TURN!

List three areas you would like to change in your life.

1. _____

2. _____

3. _____

**Next, write the positive opposite of each.
Begin each sentence with "I" or "my" to make it personal.**

Affirmations:

1. _____

2. _____

3. _____

These are your affirmations!
Don't forget to read them at least three times a day,

Remember, this isn't an activity you should only complete once if you want to see maximum growth.

Great Work!

Did you find this activity challenging?

Yes, or No? Why?

_____

_____

_____

_____

_____

_____

_____

_____

_____

_____

_____

_____

Use the next pages as journaling space.

Journaling is beneficial for improving happiness, awareness, and relieving stress.

LEARN. GROW. CHANGE.

I've learned so many great lessons in life. However, the lesson that changed the game is "Confidence is key."

Confidence is simply believing in one's own abilities or qualities.

Confidence Equation:
Good Beliefs (Faith) + Action = Positive Results

Low Self-Esteem Equation:
Negative Beliefs (Lack of Faith) + No Action = Negative Results

As a child, my mom always told my siblings and me, "Love yourself, that's enough love for everyone in the world." We would laugh and call her crazy. Well, guess who's laughing now!

Now that I can process exactly what she meant when giving us free game, I carry this knowledge with me daily.

Let's explore love and how it connects to confidence.

My description of love comes from the Bible.

⁴ **Love** is **patient**, love is **kind**. It **does not envy**, it **does not boast**, it **is not proud**.

⁵ It does **not dishonor others**, it is **not self-seeking**, it is **not easily angered**, it **keeps no record of wrongs**.

⁶ Love **does not delight in evil but rejoices with the truth**.

⁷ It **always protects, always trusts, always hopes, always perseveres**.

⁸ **Love never fails**.

1 Corinthians 13:4-8

Let's Grow!

Directions: Circle the answer choice that applies to you.

1. **Do you give yourself time to grow?**

   Yes   No   Sometimes

2. **Are you kind to yourself?**

   Yes   No   Sometimes

3. **Do you envy others? (Do you feel unhappy because someone else has achieved a goal or have a something you desire?)**

   Yes   No   Sometimes

4. **Do you compare yourself to others? (Social Media Included)**

   Yes   No   Sometimes

5. **Are you rude to yourself? (Negative Self-Talk: I'm ugly; I can't do this; I'm not good enough…)**

   Yes   No   Sometimes

Now, check your responses. Do you show yourself love?

If you realized you're not so nice to self,
that's okay if you are willing to make a change.

**This means you have room for growth!
That's why we are here.**

If you do, keep up the great work.

Moving forward, I encourage all of us to practice
loving ourselves by saying and doing the following:

I am **patient** and **kind** to myself.

I **do not envy others,** nor **do I boast about the things I have acquired. I do not think I'm better than others.**

I honor **others**. I am **not self-seeking**. I am **not easily angered**. I **forgive myself**.

I do **not laugh or celebrate negative behaviors but rejoice in positive circumstances**.

I **protect myself by doing what is always right. I trust my inner positive voice. I always hope for the best and persevere in all areas of my life.**

I never fail. For I am love.

How Does Love Play into Confidence?

Again, confidence is simply believing in one's own abilities or qualities.

The more you increase your self-love, the more you will experience a confidence boost!
Believe in your ability, your inward beauty, and your purpose in life.

Your favorite hobbies and passions in life can help you unlock your purpose in life.

Know that you were created for a reason! No one can do it like you!

Sharing your talents with the world is self-love!
Start now! Do not worry about your age or financial status.
Come with love… Confidence is love.

No one can <u>write</u> like you!
No one can <u>play the game</u> like you!
No one can <u>talk</u> like you!
No one can <u>help others</u> like you!
No one can <u>rap</u> like you!
No one can <u>play ball</u> like you!

Fill in the blank below.

No one can _____
like me!

There's only one YOU for a reason!

Be Yo(U)nique…You are the chosen one!

25

Confidence Boosters

- I got this
- Everything will work out for me
- I always come out on top
- I'm trusting the process!
- I am physically attractive
- I am confident in myself
- I love myself flaws and all
- I am confident in my abilities to accomplish my goals.

Write your own confidence boosters below.

_____

_____

_____

_____

_____

_____

_____

_____

_____

Use the next pages as journaling space.

Journaling is beneficial for improving happiness, awareness, and relieving stress.

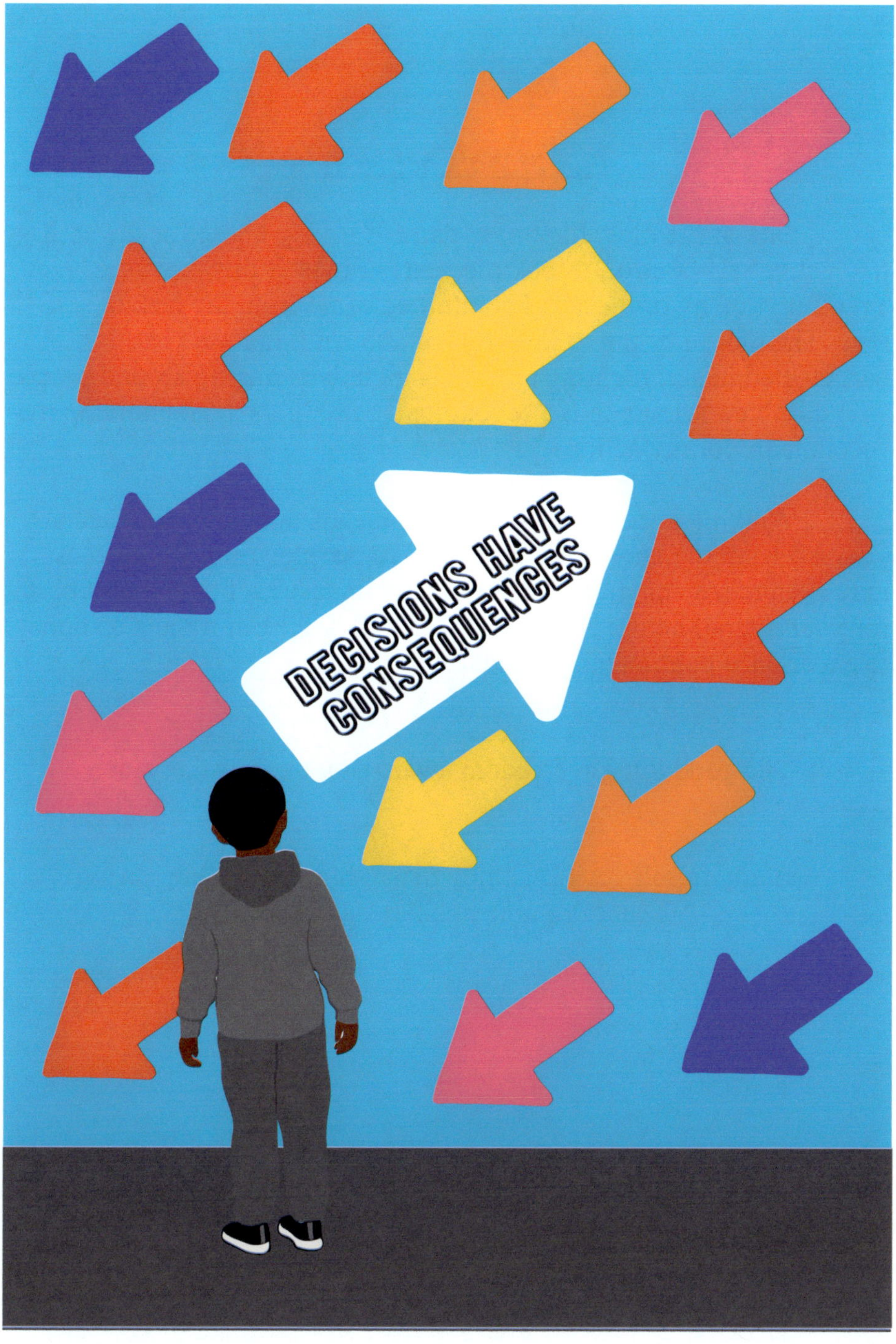
DECISIONS HAVE
CONSEQUENCES

__Part 2: Walk in Self-Love__

One of the most important parts of loving oneself is the ability to practice self-control. It took me years to master this practice. Truthfully, many of the acts I committed came from the lack of self-love. The more I began to love myself and walk in it, the less I participated in self harming acts. This included hanging around people who didn't contribute to me becoming a better person and holding me accountable for my actions.

Walking in self-love sometimes means that you must detach yourself from the habits, things, and even people you love. Also, it may even mean denying yourself of certain desires if they aren't best for your overall being. NOW THAT'S TOUGH! But it must be done to experience continuous growth.

The good thing is freedom awaits you on the other side.

Walking in self-love is simply managing and holding oneself accountable in all areas of life.

In Part 2, we will set S.M.A.R.T goals.

Remember, setting goals help us focus and develop new positive behaviors.

The results are exactly what we want: positive outcomes!

What are S.M.A.R.T goals?

S.M.A.R.T goals are:

Specific: Clear with end results

Measurable: One can track progress

Agreed: Agreed upon with everyone involved

Reasonable: Challenging yet achievable goals. (BE REAL WITH YOURSELF)

Time-Bound: Set deadline to achieve goal

Here are two examples of S.M.A.R.T goals below:

Example 1

I will earn all As in Quarter 1 next school year.

- **Specific:** The goal of earning all A's is well-defined
- **Measurable:** Success can be measured by the weekly average on graded assignments.
- **Achievable:** The goal setter will have the appropriate knowledge to achieve all A's.
- **Relevant:** The goal setter is planning to learn the content in all classes to master all assignments and test.
- **Time-based:** The goal setter has set a deadline to achieve their objective by the end of Quarter 1.

Example 2

I will earn a promotion at my job.

- **Specific:** The goal setter has clearly set the objective to be promoted to a higher position.
- **Measurable:** Success can be measured by training module completion, filing the application, and earning the promotion.
- **Achievable:** The goal setter will complete the training necessary to earn the promotion.
- **Relevant:** The goal setter is planning to apply for the promotion after finishing their training modules.
- **Time-based:** The goal setter has set a deadline to achieve their objective at the end of the following business quarter.

I set my goal on the date below:
  / /
	I achieved my goal on the date below:
	  / /

Specific: Clear with end results.	Write your goal here.
Measurable: One can track progress	Make sure it is measurable.
Agreed: Agreed upon with everyone involved	Who all does my goal involve? Do all parties agree to it?
Reasonable: Challenging yet achievable goals. Be realistic.	How does my goal challenge me? Can I get it done?
Time-Bound: Set deadline to achieve goal	What is my deadline?

I set my goal on the date below: / /	I achieved my goal on the date below: / /
Specific: Clear with end results.	Write your goal here.
Measurable: One can track progress	Make sure it is measurable.
Agreed: Agreed upon with everyone involved	Who all does my goal involve? Do all parties agree to it?
Reasonable: Challenging yet achievable goals. Be realistic.	How does my goal challenge me? Can I get it done?
Time-Bound: Set deadline to achieve goal	What is my deadline?

I set my goal on the date below: / /	I achieved my goal on the date below: / /
Specific: Clear with end results.	Write your goal here.
Measurable: One can track progress	Make sure it is measurable.
Agreed: Agreed upon with everyone involved	Who all does my goal involve? Do all parties agree to it?
Reasonable: Challenging yet achievable goals. Be realistic.	How does my goal challenge me? Can I get it done?
Time-Bound: Set deadline to achieve goal	What is my deadline?

I set my goal on the date below: / /	I achieved my goal on the date below: / /
Specific: Clear with end results.	Write your goal here.
Measurable: One can track progress	Make sure it is measurable.
Agreed: Agreed upon with everyone involved	Who all does my goal involve? Do all parties agree to it?
Reasonable: Challenging yet achievable goals. Be realistic.	How does my goal challenge me? Can I get it done?
Time-Bound: Set deadline to achieve goal	What is my deadline?

I set my goal on the date below: / /	I achieved my goal on the date below: / /
Specific: Clear with end results.	Write your goal here.
Measurable: One can track progress	Make sure it is measurable.
Agreed: Agreed upon with everyone involved	Who all does my goal involve? Do all parties agree to it?
Reasonable: Challenging yet achievable goals. Be realistic.	How does my goal challenge me? Can I get it done?
Time-Bound: Set deadline to achieve goal	What is my deadline?

I set my goal on the date below: / /	I achieved my goal on the date below: / /
Specific: Clear with end results.	Write your goal here.
Measurable: One can track progress	Make sure it is measurable.
Agreed: Agreed upon with everyone involved	Who all does my goal involve? Do all parties agree to it?
Reasonable: Challenging yet achievable goals. Be realistic.	How does my goal challenge me? Can I get it done?
Time-Bound: Set deadline to achieve goal	What is my deadline?

I set my goal on the date below:
  / /
	I achieved my goal on the date below:
	  / /

Specific: Clear with end results.	Write your goal here.
Measurable: One can track progress	Make sure it is measurable.
Agreed: Agreed upon with everyone involved	Who all does my goal involve? Do all parties agree to it?
Reasonable: Challenging yet achievable goals. Be realistic.	How does my goal challenge me? Can I get it done?
Time-Bound: Set deadline to achieve goal	What is my deadline?

I set my goal on the date below: / /	I achieved my goal on the date below: / /
Specific: Clear with end results.	Write your goal here.
Measurable: One can track progress	Make sure it is measurable.
Agreed: Agreed upon with everyone involved	Who all does my goal involve? Do all parties agree to it?
Reasonable: Challenging yet achievable goals. Be realistic.	How does my goal challenge me? Can I get it done?
Time-Bound: Set deadline to achieve goal	What is my deadline?

I set my goal on the date below:
  / /
	I achieved my goal on the date below:
	  / /

Specific: Clear with end results.	Write your goal here.
Measurable: One can track progress	Make sure it is measurable.
Agreed: Agreed upon with everyone involved	Who all does my goal involve? Do all parties agree to it?
Reasonable: Challenging yet achievable goals. Be realistic.	How does my goal challenge me? Can I get it done?
Time-Bound: Set deadline to achieve goal	What is my deadline?

Use the next pages as journaling space.

Journaling is beneficial for improving happiness, awareness, and relieving stress.

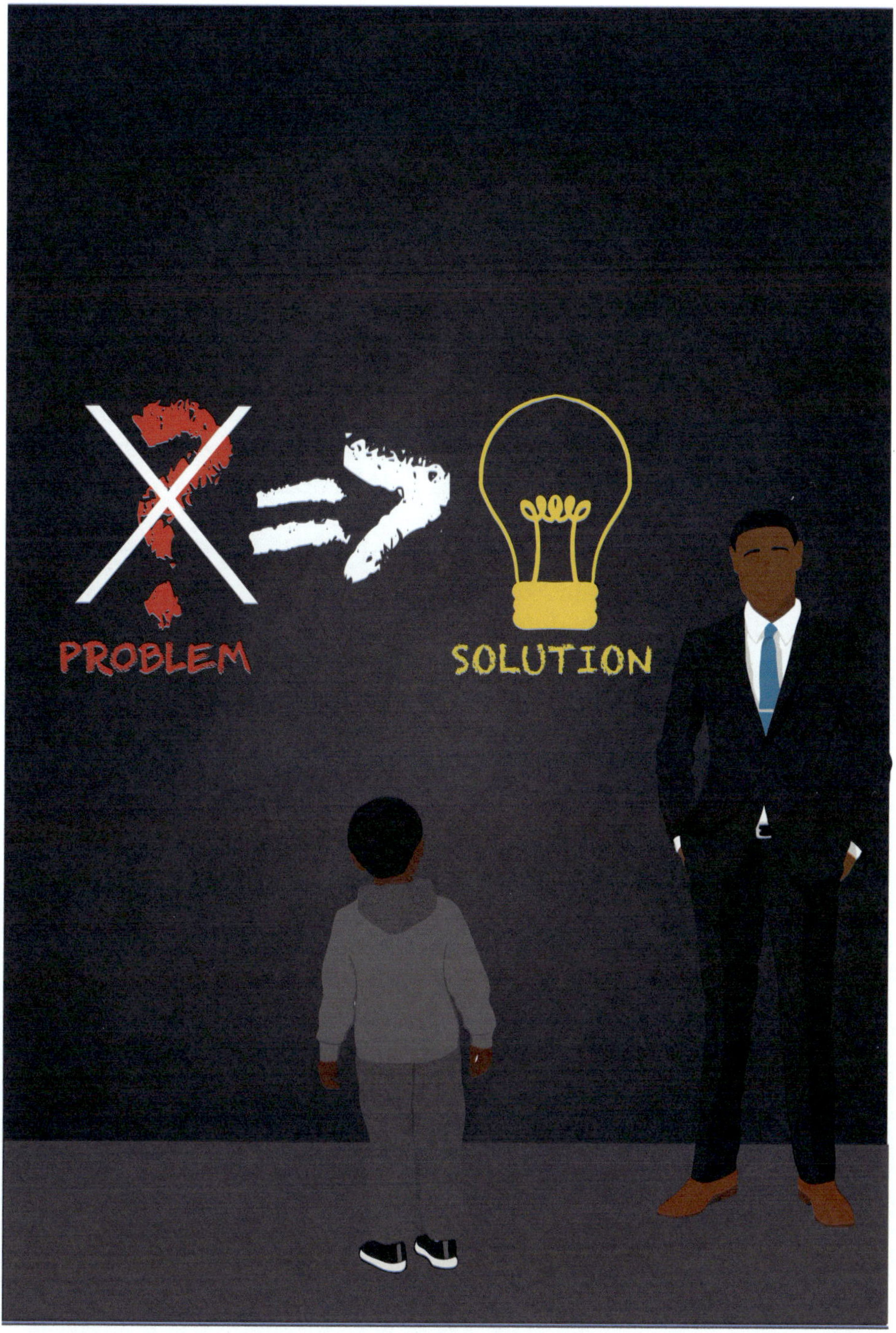
PROBLEM
SOLUTION

Part 3: Healthy Relationships

Healthy relationships you say? Now, this is an area of my life where I needed **DEEP** healing. Let me give you a piece of the back story. My loving mother has eleven children. You read it right, eleven! One can only imagine raising eleven children as a single woman with little to no help. Well, she did it with the help of my older siblings.

I am the last of the crew. So, many of my sisters helped my mother raise me. This led to me attending several schools over the years. I did not have long relationships with peers or even family members due to the instability. I learned to detach my feelings and self from people, because I felt they would eventually leave my life. Deep down, I longed for stability, consistent love, and not feeling deposable. My sisters and I jokingly called me a nomad because I moved around so much! Whew!

As an adult, I noticed the results of not healing from my childhood traumas of abandonment and rejection. Truthfully, my mother did what she thought was best for my life. It took me a very long time to understand that. So, I looked for love in all the wrong places: mainly relationships. It wasn't until I went to therapy that I realized I attracted many friends and mates with similar issues. Why am I telling you this? Well, if you are younger, I want you to evaluate the relationships in your life. Ask yourself this question "Are the people around me helping me grow in a positive way?" If you can honestly say yes, that's great! If not, leave the toxicity behind you.

Choosing healthy relationships whether it's a friendship or a mate starts early. Trust me! I've made enough mistakes for us all. One must understand forgiveness is key. We all make mistakes: some knowingly and others unknowingly. Forgive others and yourself to help attract happier and healthier relationships. Just because a person is there for you during a hardship DOES NOT make it healthy.

Here are a few tips below:

- **Choose friends wisely**. You do not have to be everyone's friend, but you should be respectful to everyone. Choose to be friends with people who build you up, not tear you down.
- **Active listening**. Listen closely to what other people are saying. Let that person know that you hear them. Ask clarifying questions. Summarize what you've heard. Though helpful, it does not always have to be through words. Eye contact and body language are also important ways of showing someone you are listening.
- **Respond carefully**. Think before you speak – especially if you are angry. Do not respond out of anger.
- **Avoid consistently giving advice or trying to fix all your friend's problems**. Only give advice when given permission, or if your friend really needs redirection to a better path.
- **Be authentic**. Be yourself. Be honest. Avoid trying to fit in. Those relationships are unhealthy and won't yield the best results.
- **Communicate openly and honestly**. Developing communication with a person can take time – and trust! Ask your friends what you can do for them. Share what you have to offer. Don't be afraid to let people know what you need. Work though issues together. Do not overstep each other's boundaries.

- **Accept your friends for who they are**. On your search for friends who can accept your authentic self, keep in mind – other people are looking for the same thing. Do not try to change your friend.
- **Respect their choices. It is okay to disagree**. If your friend decides to make a move when you think standing still is the right thing to do, let them do their thing. If you've given your advice and your friend sees things differently, step aside. What your friend is doing might be right for their life but not yours.
- **Be empathetic**. Trying to understand things from your friend's point of view can help you communicate and understand each other better.
- **Admit and apologize**. No one is perfect! When you do something wrong, admit it. Learn to apologize. Sometimes a friend is upset, and all they want from you is to (genuinely) say "sorry." Try not to make the same mistake again.
- **Let go**. Did a friend do something that hurt you? Have you talked it through? Were apologies made? Let go and move on! If you don't, you'll hang on to the transgression and it will taint the relationship going forward.
- **Keep your promises**. If you know you can't deliver something, don't promise that you will. If you make a promise, do your best to keep it. It is better to say, "I don't think I can make it Saturday, let's schedule for another time.

We all desire healthy relationships to some extent.

We must learn to move past all negative experiences to better chances on cultivating them.

Use the organizer to name problems and potential solutions in your relationships. This includes the relationships with your parents.

Use the sentence stems in the chart if needed.

*Adults, this is for you, too!

Person I would like to heal/address the relationship I have with…	
Problem The problem is…	
Potential Solution A potential solution to improve our relationship is…	

Person

I would like to heal/address the relationship I have with…

Problem

The problem is…

Potential Solution

A potential solution to improve our relationship is…

Person I would like to heal/address the relationship I have with…	
Problem The problem is…	
Potential Solution A potential solution to improve our relationship is…	

Person I would like to heal/address the relationship I have with…	
Problem The problem is…	
Potential Solution A potential solution to improve our relationship is…	

Person I would like to heal/address the relationship I have with…	
Problem The problem is…	
Potential Solution A potential solution to improve our relationship is…	

Person I would like to heal/address the relationship I have with…	
Problem The problem is…	
Potential Solution A potential solution to improve our relationship is…	

Person I would like to heal/address the relationship I have with…	
Problem The problem is…	
Potential Solution A potential solution to improve our relationship is…	

Person I would like to heal/address the relationship I have with…	
Problem The problem is…	
Potential Solution A potential solution to improve our relationship is…	

Person I would like to heal/address the relationship I have with…	
Problem The problem is…	
Potential Solution A potential solution to improve our relationship is…	

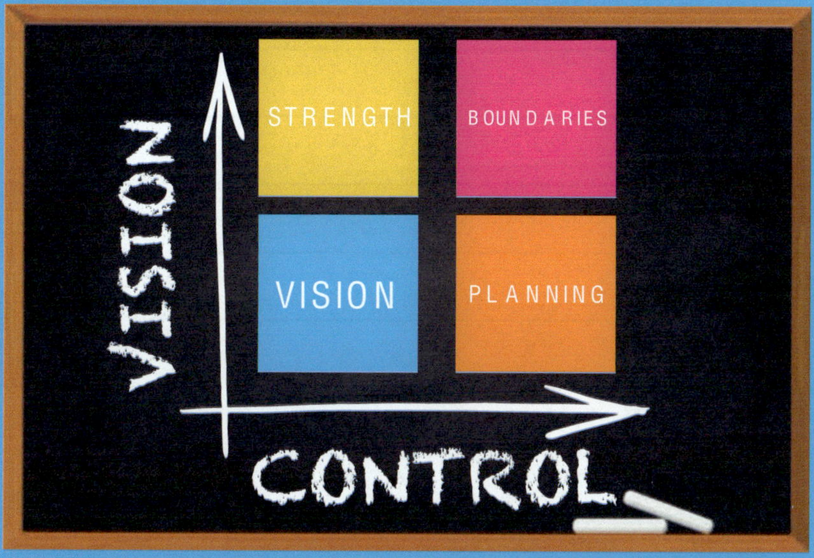
VISION
STRENGTH
BOUNDARIES
VISION
PLANNING
CONTROL

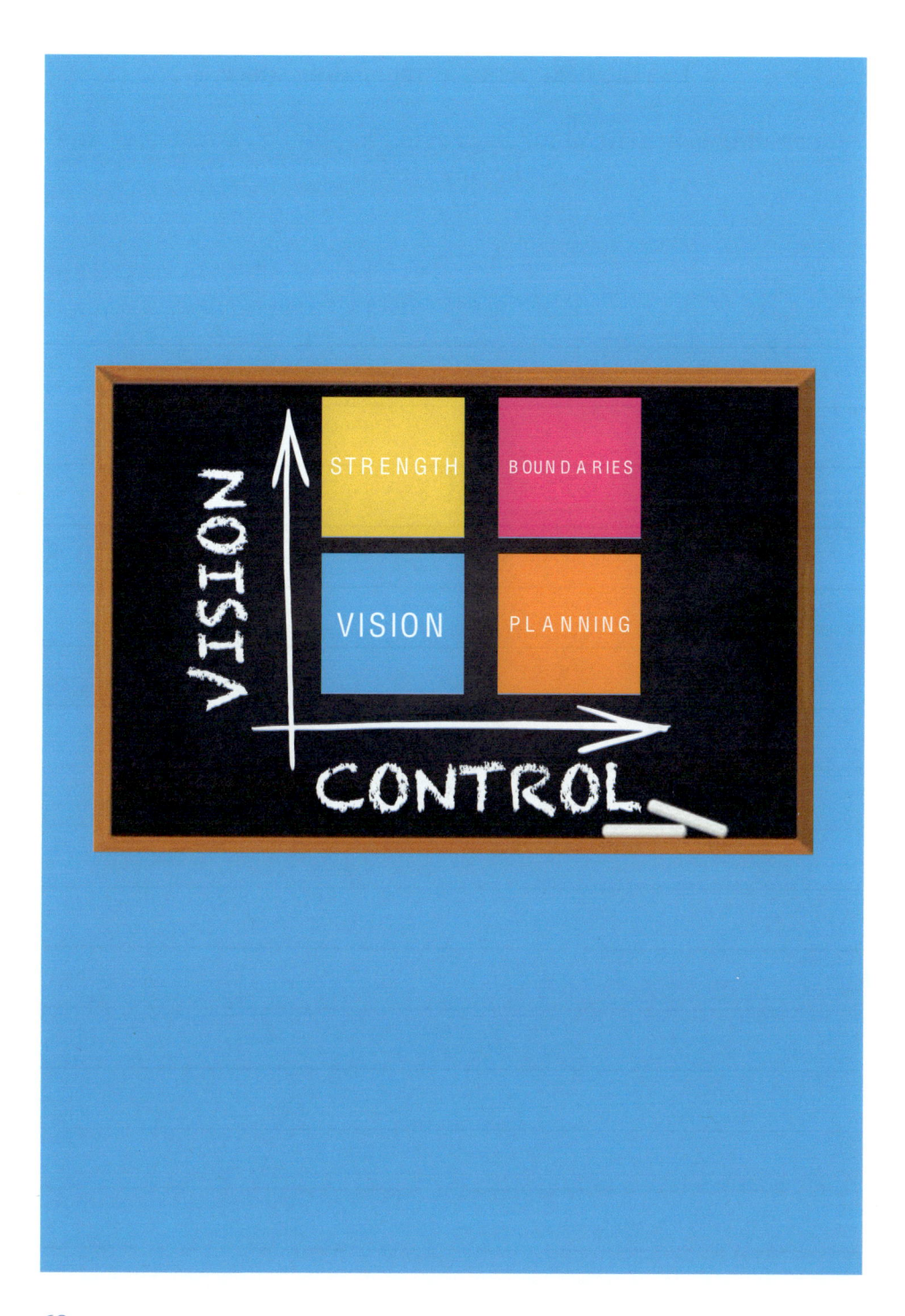

Use the next pages as journaling space.

Journaling is beneficial for improving happiness, awareness, and relieving stress.

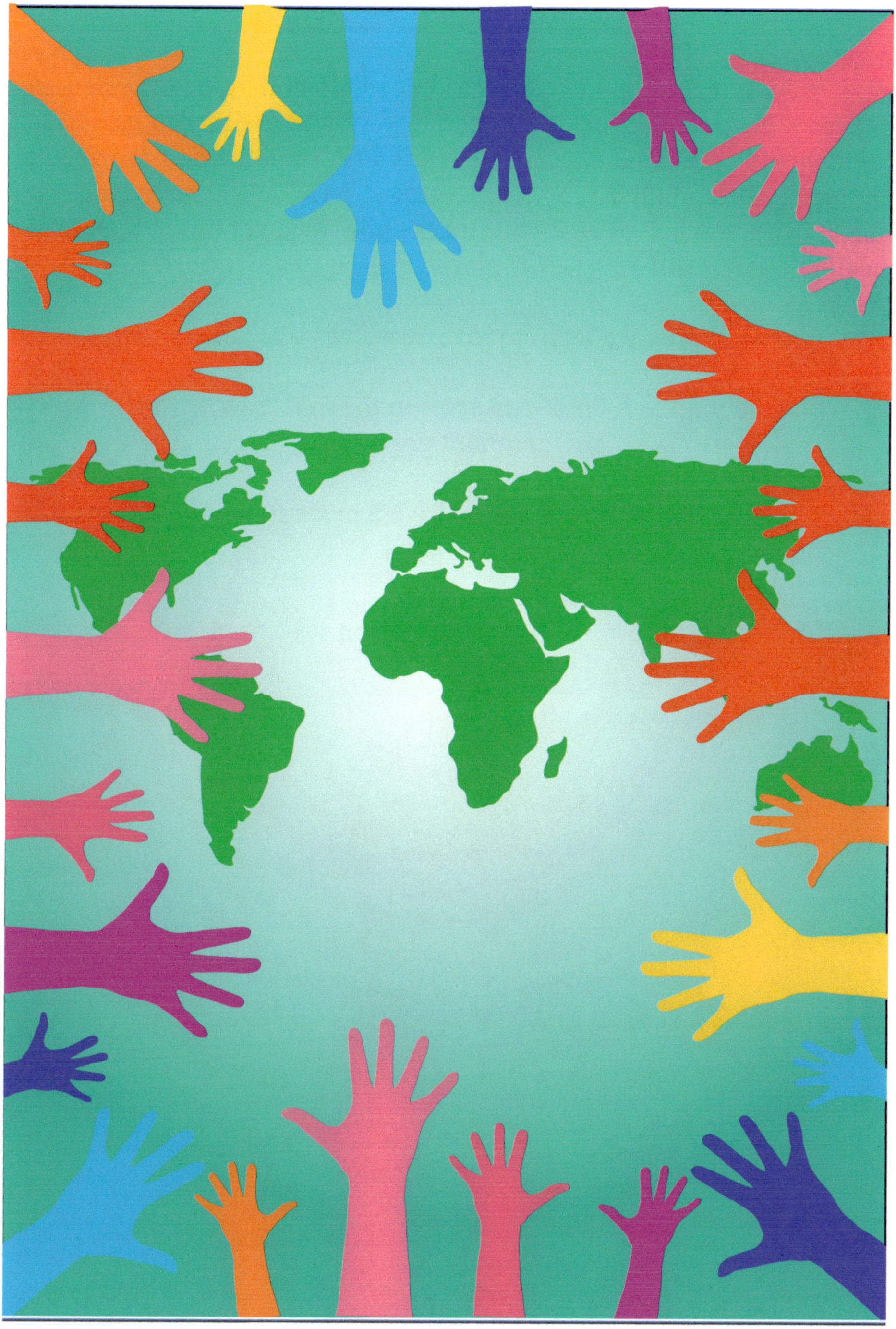

Closing: Walk in Prosperity

      As I looked in the mirror, I noticed my childhood experiences played a major role in my adulthood. I want you to develop great healing and preventive habits at an early age, so you won't have to do the work as an adult. To my adult readers, WOW! You have come so far! It is not too late to heal your inner child! WE got this. I pray total healing over us all!

I pray we learn to love ourselves like never!

We will continue to look ourselves in the mirror to self-reflect for optimum growth!

With my heart and love, I give a piece of me to you!

-April A. Wilson